A B

MW01006858

J. Newton Brown, D.D.

Containing the New Hampshire Declaration of Faith, Suggested Covenant and Rules of Order, and Brief Forms of Church Letters.

Entered according to Act of Congress, in the year 1853, by Rev. J. Newton Brown in the Clerk's Office of the District Court of the United States in and for the Eastern District of Pennsylvania.

Revised 1994

© Judson Press

Valley Forge, PA 19482-0851

Printed in the U.S.A.

94 95 96 97 98 99 00 01 02 03   41 42 43 44 45 46 47 48 49 50

Contents

Declaration of Faith: 5

I. Of the Scriptures 5

II. Of the True God 6

III. Of the Fall of Man 8

IV. Of the Way of Salvation 10

V. Of Justification 11

VI. Of the Freeness of Salvation 13

VII. Of Grace in Regeneration 14

VIII. Of Repentance and Faith 15

IX. Of God's Purpose of Grace 16

X. Of Sanctification 19

XI. Of the Perseverance of Saints 20

XII. Of the Harmony of the Law and the Gospel . . . 21

XIII. Of a Gospel Church 22

XIV. Of Baptism and the Lord's Supper 23

XV. Of the Christian Sabbath 25

XVI. Of Civil Government 26

XVII. Of the Righteous and the Wicked 27

XVIII. Of the World to Come 29

Church Covenant 31

Officers 33

Rules of Church Order 33

Forms of Church Letters 45

This Certifies That

_____

who has been baptized, on confession of faith,

was received as a member of the

_____

Baptist Church

of _____

on Sunday _____ 19_____

and the hand of fellowship given.

_____ Pastor

_____Church Clerk

Declaration of Faith

(The New Hampshire Confession of Faith as revised and enlarged by J. Newton Brown)

I. Of the Scriptures

We believe that the Holy Bible was written by men divinely inspired, and is a perfect treasure of heavenly instruction:[1] that it has God for its author, salvation for its end,[2] and truth without any mixture of error, for its matter;[3] that it reveals the principles by which God will judge us;[4] and therefore is, and shall remain to the end of the world, the true center of Christian union,[5] and the supreme standard by which all human conduct, creeds, and opinions should be tried.[6]

Places in the Bible Where Taught

[1] 2 Tim. 3:16-17—All Scripture is given by inspiration of God, and is profitable for doctrine, for reproof, for correction, for instruction in righteousness: that the man of God may be perfect, thoroughly furnished unto all good works. (Also 2 Peter 1:21; 2 Sam. 23:2; Acts 1:16; 3:21; John 10:35; Luke 16:29-31; Ps. 119:111; Rom 3:1-2.)
[2] 2 Tim. 3:15—Able to make thee wise unto salvation.

(Also 1 Peter 1:10-12; Acts 11:14; Rom. 1:16; Mark 16:16; John 5:38-39.)

[3] Prov. 30:5-6—Every word of God is pure . . . Add thou not unto his words, lest he reprove thee, and thou be found a liar. (Also John 17:17; Rev. 22:18-19; Rom. 3:4.)

[4] Rom. 2:12—As many as have sinned in the law shall be judged by the law. John 12:47-48—If any man hear my words . . . the word that I have spoken, the same shall judge him in the last day. (Also 1 Cor. 4:3-4; Luke 10:10-16; 12:47-48.)

[5] Phil. 3:16—Let us walk by the same rule, let us mind the same thing. (Also Eph. 4:3-6; Phil. 2:1-2; 1 Cor. 1:10; 1 Peter 4:11.)

[6] 1 John 4:1—Beloved, believe not every spirit, but try the spirits whether they are of God. Isa. 8:20—To the law and to the testimony: if they speak not according to this word, it is because there is no light in them. 1 Thess. 5:21—Prove all things. 2 Cor. 13:5—Prove your own selves. (Also Acts 17:11; 1 John 4:6; Jude 3; Eph. 6:17; Ps. 119:59-60; Phil. 1:9-11.)

II. Of the True God

We believe that there is one, and only one, living and true God, an infinite, intelligent Spirit, whose name is JEHOVAH, the Maker and Supreme Ruler of heaven and earth;[1] inexpressibly glorious in holiness,[2] and worthy of all possible honor, confidence, and love;[3] that in the unity of the god-head there are three persons, the Father, the Son, and the Holy Ghost;[4] equal in every divine perfection,[5] and executing distinct but harmonious offices in the great work of redemption.[6]

Places in the Bible Where Taught

[1] 1 John 4:24—God is a Spirit. Ps. 147:5—His understanding is infinite. Ps. 83:18—Thou, whose name alone is JEHOVAH, art the Most High over all the earth. (Heb. 3:4; Rom. 1:20; Jer. 10:10.)

[2] Exod. 15:11—Who is like unto thee . . . glorious in holiness. (Isa. 6:3; 1 Peter 1:15-16; Rev. 4:6-8.)

[3] Mark 12:30—Thou shalt love the Lord thy God with all thy heart, and with all thy soul, and with all thy mind, and with all thy strength. Rev. 4:11—Thou art worthy, O Lord, to receive glory and honor and power: for thou hast created all things, and for thy pleasure they are and were created. (Matt. 10:37; Jer. 2:12-13.)

[4] Matt. 28:19—Go ye therefore, and teach all nations, baptizing them in the name of the Father, and of the Son, and of the Holy Ghost. John 15:26—When the Comforter is come, whom I will send unto you from the Father, even the Spirit of truth, which proceedeth from the Father, he shall testify of me. (1 Cor. 12:4-6; 1 John 5:7.)

[5] John 10:30—I and my Father are one. (John 5:17;

14:23; 17:5,10; Acts 5:3-4; 1 Cor. 2:10-11; Phil. 2:5-6.)
[6] Eph. 2:18— For through him [the Son] we both have access by one Spirit unto the Father. 2 Cor. 13:14—The grace of the Lord Jesus Christ, and the love of God, and the communion of the Holy Ghost, be with you all. (Rev. 1:4-5; chap. 2; chap 7.)

III. Of the Fall of Man

We believe that man was created in holiness, under the law of his Maker;[1] but by voluntary transgression fell from that holy and happy state; [2] in consequence of which all mankind are now sinners;[3] not by constraint; but choice;[4] being by nature utterly void of that holiness required by the law of God, positively inclined to evil; and therefore under just condemnation to eternal ruin,[5] without defense or excuse.[6]

Places in the Bible Where Taught

[1] Gen. 1:27—God created man in his own image. Gen. 1:31—And God saw every thing that he had made, and, behold, it was very good. (Eccl. 7:29; Acts 17:26-29; Gen. 2:16-17.)
[2] Gen. 3:6-24—And when the woman saw that the tree was good for food, and that it was pleasant to the eyes, and a tree to be desired to make one wise, she took of the fruit thereof, and did eat, and gave also unto her husband

with her; and he did eat. . . . So he [the Lord God] drove out the man: and he placed at the east of the garden of Eden cherubim, and a flaming sword which turned every way, to keep the way of the tree of life. (Rom. 5:12.)

[3] Rom. 5:19—By one man's disobedience many were made sinners. (John 3:6; Ps. 51:5; Rom. 5:15-19; 8:7.)

[4] Isa. 53:6—We have turned every one to his own way. (Gen. 6:12; Rom. 3:9-18.)

[5] Eph. 2:13—. . . Among whom also we all had our conversation in times past in the lusts of our flesh, fulfilling the desires of the flesh and of the mind; and were by nature the children of wrath, even as others. Rom. 1:18—For the wrath of God is revealed from heaven against all ungodliness and unrighteousness of men, who hold the truth in unrighteousness. (Rom. 1:32; 2:1-16; Gal. 3:10; Matt. 20:15.)

[6] Ezek. 18:19-20—Yet say ye, Why? doth not the son bear the iniquity of the father? . . . The soul that sinneth, it shall die. The son shall not bear the iniquity of the father, neither shall the father bear the iniquity of the son; the righteousness of the righteous shall be upon him, and the wickedness of the wicked shall be upon him. Rom. 1:20—So that they are without excuse. Rom. 3:19—That every mouth may be stopped, and all the world may become guilty before God. (Gal. 3:22.)

IV. Of the Way of Salvation

We believe that the salvation of sinners is wholly of grace;[1] through the mediatorial offices of the Son of God; [2] who by the appointment of the Father, freely took upon him our nature, yet without sin;[3] honored the divine law by his personal obedience,[4] and by his death made a full atonement for our sins;[5] that having risen from the dead he is now enthroned in heaven;[6] and uniting in his wonderful person the tenderest sympathies with divine perfections, he is every way qualified to be a suitable, a compassionate, and an all-sufficient Saviour.[7]

Places in the Bible Where Taught

[1] Eph. 2:8—By grace are ye saved. (Matt. 18:11; 1 John 4:10; 1 Cor. 3:5,7; Acts 15:11.)

[2] John 3:16—For God so loved the world, that he gave his only begotten Son, that whosoever believeth in him should not perish, but have everlasting life. (John 1:1-14; Heb. 4:14; 12:24.)

[3] Phil. 2:6-7—Who, being in the form of God, thought it not robbery to be equal with God: but made himself of no reputation, and took upon him the form of a servant, and was made in the likeness of men. (Heb. 2:9,14; 2 Cor. 5:21.)

[4] Isa. 42:21. The Lord is well pleased for his righteousness' sake; he will magnify the law, and make it honor-

able. (Phil. 2:8; Gal. 4:4-5; Rom. 3:21.)

[5] Isa. 53:4-5—. . . He was wounded for our transgressions, he was bruised for our iniquities: the chastisement of our peace was upon him; and with his stripes we are healed. (Matt. 20:28; Rom. 4:25; 3:21-26; 1 John 4:10; 2:2; 1 Cor. 15:1-3; Heb. 9:13-15.)

[6] Heb. 1:8—Unto the Son he saith, Thy throne, O God, is for ever and ever. (Heb. 1:3; 8:1; Col. 3:1-4.)

[7] Heb. 7:25—Wherefore he is able also to save them to the uttermost that come unto God by him, seeing he ever liveth to make intercession for them. Col. 2:9—For in him dwelleth all the fulness of the Godhead bodily. Heb. 2:18—In that he himself hath suffered being tempted, he is able to succor them that are tempted. (Heb. 7:26; Ps. 89:19; Ps. 34.)

V. Of Justification

We believe that the great gospel blessing which Christ[1] secures to such as believe in him is justification;[2] that justification includes the pardon of sin,[3] and the promise of eternal life on principles of righteousness;[4] that it is bestowed, not in consideration of any works of righteousness which we have done, but solely through faith in the Redeemer's blood;[5] by virtue of which faith his perfect righteousness is freely imputed to us of God;[6] that it brings us into a state of most blessed peace and favor with God, and secures every other blessing needful for time and eternity.[7]

Places in the Bible Where Taught

[1] John 1:26—Of his fulness have all we received. (Eph. 3:8.)

[2] Acts 13:39—By him all that believe are justified from all things. (Isa. 53:11-12; Rom. 8:1.)

[3] Rom. 5:9—Being now justified by his blood, we shall be saved from wrath through him. (Zech. 13:1; Matt. 9:6; Acts 10:43.)

[4] Rom. 5:17—They which receive abundance of grace and of the gift of righteousness shall reign in life by one, Jesus Christ. (Titus 3:5-7; 1 Peter 3:7; 1 John 2:25; Rom. 5:21.)

[5] Rom. 4:4-5—Now to him that worketh is the reward not reckoned of grace, but of debt. But to him that worketh not, but believeth on him that justifieth the ungodly, his faith is counted for righteousness. (Rom. 5:21; 6:23; Phil. 3:7-9.)

[6] Rom. 5:19—By the obedience of one shall many be made righteous. (Rom. 3:24-26; 4:23-25; 1 John 2:12.)

[7] Rom. 5:1-2—Being justified by faith, we have peace with God through our Lord Jesus Christ: by whom also we have access by faith into this grace wherein we stand, and rejoice in hope of the glory of God. Rom. 5:3—We

glory in tribulations also. Rom. 5:11—We also joy in God. (1 Cor. 1:30-31; Matt. 6:33; 1 Tim. 4:8.)

VI. Of the Freeness of Salvation

We believe that the blessings of salvation are made free to all by the gospel;[1] that it is the immediate duty of all to accept them by a cordial, penitent, and obedient faith;[2] and that nothing prevents the salvation of the greatest sinner on earth but his own inherent depravity and voluntary rejection of the gospel;[3] which rejection involves him in an aggravated condemnation.[4]

Places in the Bible Where Taught

[1] Isa. 55:1—Ho, every one that thirsteth, come ye to the waters. Rev. 22:17—Whatsoever will let him take the water of life freely. (Luke 14:17.)

[2] Rom. 16:25-26—My gospel . . . according to the commandment of the everlasting God, made known to all nations for the obedience of faith. (Mark 1:15; Rom. 1:15-17.)

[3] John 5:40—Ye will not come to me, that ye might have life. (Matt. 23:37; Rom. 9:32; Prov. 1:24; Acts 13:46.)

[4] John 3:19—And this is the condemnation, that light is come into the world, and men loved darkness rather than light, because their deeds were evil. (Matt. 11:20; Luke 19:27; 2 Thess. 1:8.)

VII. Of Grace in Regeneration

We believe that, in order to be saved, sinners must be regenerated or born again;[1] that regeneration consists in giving a holy disposition to the mind;[2] that it is effected, in a manner above our comprehension, by the power of the Holy Spirit in connection with divine truth,[3] so as to secure our voluntary obedience to the gospel;[4] and that its proper evidence appears in the holy fruits of repentance and faith and newness of life.[5]

Places in the Bible Where Taught

[1] John 3:3—Verily, verily, I say unto thee, Except a man be born again, he cannot see the kingdom of God. (John 3:6-7; 1 Cor. 1:14; Rev. 14:3; 21:27.)

[2] 2 Cor. 5:17—If any man be in Christ, he is a new creature. (Ezek. 36:26; Deut. 30:6; Rom. 2:28-29; 5:5; 1 John 4:7.)

[3] John 3:8—The wind bloweth where it listeth, and thou hearest the sound thereof, but canst not tell whence it cometh, and whither it goeth: so is every one that is born of the Spirit. John 1:13—Which were born, not of blood, nor of the will of the flesh, nor of the will of man, but of God. James 1:16-18—. . . Of his own will begat he us with the word of truth. (1 Cor. 1:30; Phil. 2:13.)

[4] 1 Peter 1:22-25—Ye have purified your souls in obeying the truth through the Spirit. 1 John 5:1—Whosoever

believeth that Jesus is the Christ is born of God. (Eph. 4:20-24; Col. 3:9-11.)

[5] Eph. 5:9—The fruit of the Spirit is in all goodness and righteousness and truth. (Rom. 8:9; Gal. 5:16-23; Eph. 2:14-21; Matt. 3:8-10; 7:20; 1 John 5:4,18.)

VIII. Of Repentance and Faith

We believe that repentance and faith are sacred duties, and also inseparable graces, wrought in our souls by the regenerating Spirit of God;[1] whereby, being deeply convinced of our guilt, danger, and helplessness, and of the way of salvation by Christ,[2] we turn to God with unfeigned contrition, confession, and supplication for mercy;[3] at the same time heartily receiving the Lord Jesus Christ as our Prophet, Priest, and King, and relying on him alone as the only and all-sufficient Saviour.[4]

Places in the Bible Where Taught

[1] Mark 1:15—Repent ye, and believe the gospel. Acts 11:18—Then hath God also to the Gentiles granted repentance unto life. Eph. 2:8—By grace are ye saved through faith; and that not of yourselves: it is the gift of God. 1 John 5:1— Whosoever believeth that Jesus is the Christ is born of God.

[2] John 16:8—He will reprove the world of sin, and of righteousness, and of judgment. Acts 2:37-38—They

were pricked in their heart, and said . . . Men and brethren, what shall we do? Then Peter said unto them, Repent, and be baptized every one of you in the name of
Jesus Christ for the remission of sins. (Acts 16:30-31.)
[3] Luke 18:13—And the publican . . . smote upon his
breast, saying, God be merciful to me a sinner. (Luke
15:18-21; James 4:7-10; 2 Cor. 7:11; Rom. 10:12-13; Ps.
51.)
[4] Rom. 10:9-11—If thou shalt confess with thy mouth the
Lord Jesus, and shalt believe in thine heart that God hath
raised him from the dead, thou shalt be saved. (Acts 3:22-
23; Heb. 4:14; Ps. 2:6; Heb. 1:8; 7:25, 2 Tim. 1:12.)

IX. Of God's Purpose of Grace

We believe that election is the eternal purpose of God, according to which he graciously regenerates, sanctifies,
and saves sinners;[1] that being perfectly consistent with
the free agency of man, it comprehends all the means in
connection with the end;[2] that it is a most glorious dis-
play of God's sovereign goodness, being infinitely free,
wise, holy, and unchangeable;[3] that it utterly excludes
boasting, and promotes humility, love, prayer, praise,
trust in God, and active imitation of his free mercy;[4] that
it encourages the use of means in the highest degree;[5]
that it may be ascertained by its effects in all who truly
believe the gospel;[6] that it is the foundation of Christian

assurance;[7] and that to ascertain it with regard to ourselves demands and deserves the utmost diligence.[8]

Places in the Bible Where Taught

[1] 2 Tim. 1:8-9—Be not therefore ashamed of the testimony of our Lord, nor of me his prisoner: but be thou partaker of the afflictions of the gospel, according to the power of God: who hath saved us, and called us with a holy calling, not according to our works, but according to his own purpose and grace, which was given us in Christ Jesus before the world began. (Eph. 1:3-14; 1 Peter 1:1-2; Rom. 11:5-6; John 15:16; 1 John 4:19.)

[2] 2 Thess. 2:13-14—But we are bound to give thanks always to God for you, brethren beloved of the Lord, because God hath from the beginning chosen you to salvation through sanctification of the Spirit and belief of the truth: whereunto he called you by our gospel, to the obtaining of the glory of our Lord Jesus Christ. (Acts 13:48; John 10:16; Matt. 20:16; Acts 15:14.)

[3] Exod. 33:18-19—And he [Moses] said, I beseech thee, shew me thy glory. And he said, I will make all my goodness pass before thee, and I will proclaim the name of the LORD before thee; and will be gracious to whom I will be gracious, and will shew mercy on whom I will shew mercy. Matt. 20:15—Is it not lawful for me to do what I will with mine own? Is thine eye evil, because I am

good? (Eph. 1:11; Rom. 9:23-24; Jer. 31:3; Rom. 11:28-29; James 1:17-18; 2 Tim. 1:9; Rom. 11:32-36.)

⁴ 1 Cor. 4:7—For who maketh thee to differ from another? And what hast thou that thou didst not receive? Now if thou didst receive it, why dost thou glory, as if thou hadst not received it? (1 Cor. 1:26-31; Rom. 3:27; 4:16; Col. 3:12; 1 Cor. 15:10; 1 Peter 5:10; 1 Thess. 2:12-13; 1 Peter 2:9; Luke 18:7.)

⁵ 2 Tim. 2:10—Therefore I endure all things for the elect's sake, that they may also obtain the salvation which is in Christ Jesus with eternal glory. 1 Cor. 9:22—I am made all things to all men, that I might by all means save some. (John 6:37-40; 2 Peter 1:10.)

⁶ 1 Thess. 1:4-10—Knowing, brethren beloved, your election of God. For our gospel came not unto you in word only, but also in power, and in the Holy Ghost, and in much assurance.

⁷ Rom. 8:28-31—Moreover, whom he did predestinate, them he also called: and whom he called, them he also justified: and whom he justified, them he also glorified. What shall we then say to these things? If God be for us, who can be against us? (Isa. 42:16; Rom. 11:29.)

⁸ 2 Peter 1:10-11—Wherefore the rather, brethren, give diligence to make your calling and election sure: for if ye do these things, we shall never fall: for so an entrance shall be ministered unto you abundantly into the everlast-

ing kingdom of our Lord and Saviour Jesus Christ. (Phil. 3:12; Heb. 6:11.)

X. Of Sanctification

We believe that sanctification is the process by which, according to the will of God, we are made partakers of his holiness;[1] that it is a progressive work;[2] that it is begun in regeneration;[3] and that it is carried on in the hearts of believers by the presence and power of the Holy Spirit, the Sealer and Comforter, in the continual use of the appointed means, especially the word of God, self-examination, self-denial, watchfulness, and prayer.[4]

Places in the Bible Where Taught

[1] 1 Thess. 4:3—For this is the will of God, even your sanctification. 1 Thess. 5:23—And the very God of peace sanctify you wholly. (2 Cor. 7:1; 13:9; Eph 1:4.)

[2] Prov. 4:18—The path of the just is as the shining light, that shineth more and more unto the perfect day. (Heb. 6:1; 2 Peter 1:5-8; Phil. 3:12-16.)

[3] 1 John 2:29—If ye know that he [God] is righteous, ye know that every one that doeth righteousness is born of him. Rom. 8:5—They that are after the flesh do mind the things of the flesh; but they that are after the Spirit, the things of the Spirit. (John 3:6; Phil. 1:9-11.)

[4] Phil. 2:12-13—Work out your own salvation with fear

and trembling: for it is God which worketh in you both to will and to do of his good pleasure. (Eph. 4:11-12,30; 6:18; 1 Peter 2:2; 2 Peter 3:18; 2 Cor. 13:5; Luke 9:23; 11:35; Matt. 26:41; Eph. 6:18.)

XI. Of the Perseverance of Saints

We believe that such only are real believers as endure unto the end;[1] that their persevering attachment to Christ is the grand mark which distinguishes them from superficial professors;[2] that a special Providence watches over their welfare;[3] and that they are kept by the power of God through faith unto salvation.[4]

Places in the Bible Where Taught

[1] John 8:31—Then said Jesus, . . . If ye continue in my word, then are ye my disciples indeed. (1 John 2:27-28; 3:9; 5:18.)

[2] 1 John 2:19—They went out from us, but they were not of us; for if they had been of us, they would no doubt have continued with us: but they went out, that they might be made manifest that they were not all of us. (John 13:18; Matt. 13:20-21; John 6:66-69.)

[3] Rom. 8:28—And we know that all things work together for good to them that love God, to them who are the called according to his purpose. (Matt. 6:30-33; Jer. 32:40; Ps. 121:2; 91:11-12.)

[4] Phil. 1:6—He which hath begun a good work in you will perform it until the day of Jesus Christ. (Phil. 2:12-13; Jude 24-25; Heb. 1:14; 13:5; 1 John 4:4.)

XII. Of the Harmony of the Law and the Gospel

We believe that the Law of God is the eternal and unchangeable rule of his moral government;[1] that it is holy, just, and good;[2] and that the inability which the Scriptures ascribe to fallen men to fulfil its precepts arises entirely from their love of sin;[3] to deliver them from which, and to restore them through a Mediator to unfeigned obedience to the holy Law, is one great end of the gospel, and of the means of grace connected with the establishment of the visible church.[4]

Places in the Bible Where Taught

[1] Rom. 3:31—Do we then make void the law through faith? God forbid: yea, we establish the law. (Matt. 5:17; Luke 16:17; Rom. 3:20; 4:15.)

[2] Rom. 7:12—The law is holy, and the commandment holy, and just, and good. (Rom. 7:7,14,22; Gal. 3:21; Ps. 119.)

[3] Rom. 8:7-8—The carnal mind is enmity against God: for it is not subject to the law of God, neither indeed can be. So then they that are in the flesh cannot please God. (Josh. 24:19; Jer. 13:23; John 6:44; 5:44.)

[4] Rom. 8:2-4—For the law of the spirit of life in Christ Jesus hath made me free from the law of sin and death. For what the law could not do, in that it was weak through the flesh, God sending his own Son in the likeness of sinful flesh, and for sin, condemned sin in the flesh: that the righteousness of the law might be fulfilled in us, who walk not after the flesh, but after the Spirit. (Rom. 10:4; Heb. 8:10; 12:14; Jude 20-21.)

XIII. Of a Gospel Church

We believe that a visible church of Christ is a congregation of baptized believers,[1] associated by covenant in the faith and fellowship of the gospel;[2] observing the ordinances of Christ;[3] governed by his laws;[4] and exercising the gifts, rights, and privileges invested in them by his word;[5] that its only Scriptural officers are bishops, or pastors, and deacons,[6] whose qualifications, claims, and duties are defined in the epistles to Timothy and Titus.

Places in the Bible Where Taught

[1] 1 Cor. 1:1-13—Paul . . . unto the church of God which is at Corinth . . . Is Christ divided? was Paul crucified for you? or were ye baptized in the name of Paul? (Matt. 18:17; Acts 5:11; 8:1; 11:21-23; 1 Cor. 4:17; 14:23; 3 John 9.)

[2] Acts 2:41-42—When they that gladly received his word

were baptized: and the same day there were added unto them about three thousand souls. 2 Cor. 8:5—They . . . first gave their own selves to the Lord, and unto us by the will of God. (Acts 2:47; 1 Cor. 5:12-13.)

[3] 1 Cor. 11:2—Now I praise you, brethren, that ye remember me in all things, and keep the ordinances, as I delivered them to you. (2 Thess. 3:6; Rom. 16:17-20; 1 Cor. 11:23-34; Matt. 18:15-20; 2 Cor. 2:17; 1 Cor. 4:17.)

[4] Matt. 28:20—Teaching them to observe all things whatsoever I have commanded you. (John 14:15; 15:12; 1 John 4:21; John 14:21; 1 Thess. 4:2; 2 John 6; Gal. 6:2; all the Epistles.)

[5] Eph. 4:7—Unto every one of us is given grace according to the measure of the gift of Christ. 1 Cor. 14:12—Seek that ye may excel to the edifying of the church. Phil. 1:27—That . . . I may hear of your affairs, that ye stand fast in one spirit, and one mind striving together for the faith of the gospel.

[6] Phil. 1:1—With the bishops and deacons. (Acts 14:23; 15:22; 1 Tim. 3; Titus 1.)

XIV. Of Baptism and the Lord's Supper

We believe that Christian baptism is the immersion in water of a believer,[1] into the name of the Father, and Son, and Holy Ghost;[2] to show forth, in a solemn and beautiful emblem, our faith in the crucified, buried, and risen Saviour, with its effect in our death to sin and resurrection to a new life;[3] that it is prerequisite to the privileges of a church relation; and to the Lord's Supper;[4] in which the members of the church, by the sacred use of bread and wine are to commemorate together the dying love of Christ;[5] preceded always by solemn self-examination.[6]

Places in the Bible Where Taught

[1] Acts 8:36-39—And the eunuch said, See, here is water; what doth hinder me to be baptized? And Philip said, If thou believest with all thine heart, thou mayest. . . . And they went down both into the water, both Philip and the eunuch; and he baptized him. (Matt. 3:5-6; John 3:22-23; 4:1-2; Matt. 28:19; Mark 16:16; Acts 2:38; 8:12; 16:32-34; 18:8.)

[2] Matt. 28:19—Baptizing them in the name of the Father, and of the Son, and of the Holy Ghost. (Acts 10:47-48; Gal. 3:27-28.)

[3] Rom. 6:4—Therefore we are buried with him by baptism into death: that like as Christ was raised up from the dead by the glory of the Father, even so we also should walk in newness of life. (Col. 2:12; 1 Peter 3:20-21; Acts 22:16.)

[4] Acts 2:41-42—Then they that gladly received his word were baptized: and the same day there were added unto them about three thousand souls. And they continued

steadfastly in the apostles' doctrine and fellowship, and in breaking of bread, and in prayers. (Matt. 28:19-20; Acts and Epistles.)

[5] 1 Cor. 11:26—As often as ye eat this bread, and drink this cup, ye do shew the Lord's death till he come. (Matt. 26:26-29; Mark 14:22-25; Luke 22:14-20.)

[6] 1 Cor. 11:28—But let a man examine himself, and so let him eat of that bread, and drink of that cup. (1 Cor. 5:1,8; 10:3-32; 11:17-32; John 6:26-71.)

XV. Of the Christian Sabbath

We believe that the first day of the week is the Lord's Day, or Christian Sabbath;[1] and is to be kept sacred to religious purposes,[2] by abstaining from all secular labor and sinful recreation;[3] by the devout observance of all the means of grace, both private[4] and public;[5] and by preparation for that rest that remaineth for the people of God.[6]

Places in the Bible Where Taught

[1] Acts 20:7—Upon the first day of the week, when the disciples came together to break bread, Paul preached unto them. (Gen. 2:3; Col. 2:16-17; Mark 2:27; John 20:19; 1 Cor. 16:1-2.)

[2] Exod. 20:8—Remember the sabbath day, to keep it holy. Rev. 1:10—I was in the Spirit of the Lord's Day. Ps. 118:24—This is the day which the Lord hath made; we

will rejoice and be glad in it.

[3] Isa. 58:13-14—If thou turn away thy foot from the sabbath, from doing thy pleasure on my holy day; and call the sabbath a delight, the holy of the LORD, honorable; and shalt honor him, not doing thine own ways, nor finding thine own pleasure, nor speaking thine own words: then shalt thou delight thyself in the LORD; and I will cause thee to ride upon the high places of the earth, and feed thee with the heritage of Jacob.

[4] Ps. 118:15—The voice of rejoicing and salvation is in the tabernacles of the righteous.

[5] Heb. 1:24-25—. . . Not forsaking the assembling of ourselves together, as the manner of some is. Acts 11:26—A whole year they assembled themselves with the church, and taught much people.

[6] Heb. 4:3-11—Let us labor therefore to enter into that rest.

XVI. Of Civil Government

We believe that civil government is of divine appointment, for the interests and good order of human society;[1] and that magistrates are to be prayed for, conscientiously honored and obeyed;[2] except only in things opposed to the will of our Lord Jesus Christ,[3] who is the only Lord of the conscience, and the Prince of the kings of the earth.[4]

Places in the Bible Where Taught

[1] Rom. 13:1-7—The powers that be are ordained by God. . . . For rulers are not a terror to good works, but to the evil. (Deut. 16:18; 2 Sam. 23:3; Exod. 18:21-23; Jer. 30:21.)

[2] Matt. 22:21—Render therefore unto Caesar the things which are Caesar's; and unto God the things that are God's. (Titus 3:1; 1 Peter 2:13; 1 Tim. 3:1-3.)

[3] Acts 5:29—We ought to obey God rather than men. Matt. 10:28—Fear not them which kill the body, but are not able to kill the soul. (Dan. 3:15-18; 6:7-10; Acts 4:18-20.)

[4] Matt. 23:10—One is your Master, even Christ. Rom. 14:4—Who art thou that judgest another man's servant? Rev. 19:16—And he hath on his vesture and on his thigh a name written, KING OF KINGS, AND LORD OF LORDS. (Ps. 72:11; Ps. 2; Rom. 14:9-13.)

XVII. Of the Righteous and the Wicked

We believe that there is a radical and essential difference between the righteous and the wicked;[1] that such only as through faith are justified in the name of the Lord Jesus, and sanctified by the Spirit of our God, are truly righteous in his esteem;[2] while all such as continue in impenitence and unbelief are in his sight wicked, and under the curse;[3] and this distinction holds among men both in and after death.[4]

Places in the Bible Where Taught

[1] Mal. 3:18—Then shall ye return, and discern between the righteous and the wicked, between him that serveth God and him that serveth him not. (Prov. 12:26; Isa. 5:20; Gen. 18:23; Acts 10:34-35; Rom. 6:16.)

[2] Rom. 1:27—The just shall live by faith. Rom. 7:6—We are delivered from the law, that being dead wherein we were held; that we should serve in newness of spirit, and not in the oldness of the letter. 1 John 2:29—If ye know that he is righteous, ye know that every one that doeth righteousness is born of him. (1 John 3:7; Rom. 6:18,22; 1 Cor. 11:32; Prov. 11:31; 1 Peter 4:17-18.)

[3] 1 John 5:19—And we know that we are of God, and the whole world lieth in wickedness. Gal. 3:10—As many as are of the works of the law, are under the curse. (John 3:36; Isa. 57:21; Ps. 10:4; Isa. 55:6-7.)

[4] Prov. 14:32—The wicked is driven away in his wickedness: but the righteous hath hope in his death. *See also, the example of the rich man and Lazarus.* Luke 16:25—Thou in thy lifetime receivedst thy good things, and likewise Lazarus evil things: but now he is comforted, and thou art tormented. (John 8:21-14; Prov. 10:24; Luke 12:4-5; 9:23-26; John 12:25-26; Eccl. 3:17; Matt. 7:13-14.)

XVIII. Of the World to Come

We believe that the end of the world is approaching;[1] that at the last day Christ will descend from heaven,[2] and raise the dead from the grave to final retribution;[3] that a solemn separation will then take place;[4] that the wicked will be adjudged to endless punishment, and the righteous to endless joy;[5] and that this judgment will fix forever the final state of men in heaven or hell, on principles of righteousness.

Places in the Bible Where Taught

[1] 1 Peter 4:7—But the end of all things is at hand: be ye therefore sober, and watch unto prayer. (1 Cor. 7:29-31; Heb. 1:10-12; Matt. 25:31; 28:20; 13:39-43; 1 John 2:17; 2 Peter 3:3-13.)

[2] Acts 1:11—This same Jesus, which was taken up from you into heaven, shall so come in like manner as ye have seen him go into heaven. (Rev. 1:7; Heb. 9:28; Acts 3:21; 1 Thess. 4:13-18; 5:1-11.)

[3] Acts 24:15—There shall be a resurrection of the dead, both of the just and the unjust. (1 Cor. 15:12-58; Luke 14:14; Dan. 12:2; John 5:28-29; 6:40; 11:25-26; Acts 10:42.)

[4] Matt. 13:49—The angels shall come forth, and sever the wicked from among the just. (Matt. 13:37-43; 24:30-31; 25:31-33.)

[5] Matt. 25:31-46—And these shall go away into everlasting punishment: but the righteous into life eternal. Rev. 22:11—He that is unjust, let him be unjust still: and he which is filthy, let him be filthy still: and he that is righteous, let him be righteous still: and he that is holy let him be holy still. (1 Cor. 6:9-10; Mark 9:43-48; 2 Peter 2:9; Jude 7; Phil. 3:19; Rom. 6:23; 2 Cor. 5:10-11; John 4:36; 2 Cor. 4:18.)

[6] Rom. 3:5-6—Is God unrighteous who taketh vengeance? (I speak as a man) God forbid: for how then shall God judge the world? 2 Thess. 1:6-12—Seeing it is a righteous thing with God to recompense tribulation to them that trouble you, and to you who are troubled rest with us . . . when he shall come to be glorified in his saints, and to be admired in all them that believe. (Heb. 6:1-2; 1 Cor. 4:5; Acts 17:31; Rom. 2:2-16; Rev. 20:11-12; 1 John 2:28; 4:17.)

2 Peter 3:11-12—Seeing then that all these things shall be dissolved, what manner of persons ought ye to be in all holy conversation and godliness, looking for and hasting unto the coming of the day of God. . . ?

Church Covenant

Having been led, as we believe, by the Spirit of God to receive the Lord Jesus Christ as our Saviour; and, on the profession of our faith, having been baptized in the name of the Father, and of the Son, and of the Holy Spirit, we do now, in the presence of God, angels, and this assembly, most solemnly and joyfully enter into covenant with one another, as one body in Christ.

We engage, therefore, by the aid of the Holy Spirit, to walk together in Christian love; to strive for the advancement of this church, in knowledge, holiness, and comfort; to promote its prosperity and spirituality; to sustain its worship, ordinances, discipline, and doctrines; to contribute cheerfully and regularly to the support of the ministry, the expenses of the church, the relief of the poor, and the spread of the gospel through all nations.

We also engage to maintain family and secret devotions; to religiously educate our children; to seek the salvation of our kindred and acquaintances; to walk circumspectly in the world; to be just in our dealings, faithful in our engagements, and exemplary in our deportment; to avoid all tattling, backbiting, and excessive anger; to abstain from the sale and use of intoxicating drinks as a beverage; and to be zealous in our efforts to advance the kingdom of our Saviour.

We further engage to watch over one another in Christian love; to remember each other in prayer; to aid each other in sickness and distress; to cultivate Christian sympathy in feeling and courtesy in speech; to be slow to take offense, but always ready for reconciliation, and mindful of the rules of our Saviour, to secure it without delay.

We moreover engage, that when we remove from this place, we will as soon as possible unite with some other church, where we can carry out the spirit of this covenant and the principles of God's Word.

Prayer

Now the God of peace, who brought again from the dead our Lord Jesus, that Great Shepherd of the sheep, through the blood of the everlasting covenant, make you perfect in every good work to do his will; working in you that which is well pleasing in his sight, through Jesus Christ to whom be glory for ever and ever. Amen.

Officers

Pastor _____

Deacons _____

_____

_____

Clerk _____

Treasurer _____

Rules of Church Order

Let all things be done decently and in order (1 Corinthians 14:40).

Let all things be done with charity (1 Corinthians 16:14).

Let all things be done unto edifying (1 Corinthians 14:26).

Do all in the name of the Lord Jesus (Colossians 3:17).

ART. I. Reception of Members

Sec. 1. Any person professing faith in the Lord Jesus Christ, giving evidence of a change of heart, and adopting the views of faith and practice held by this church as set forth in the foregoing declaration, may, upon baptism, be received into its membership.

Sec. 2. Candidates for baptism shall be examined before the church; and their admission shall not be acted on until the church has ascertained their character and standing. It is desirable that the question of reception shall not be taken in their presence.

Sec. 3. Members from other churches holding the same faith may be received by letters of recommendation and dismission from their respective churches.

Sec. 4. Those who have once been members of Baptist churches, and in consequence of any peculiar circumstances have no regular letters of dismission, may be received by giving satisfactory evidence of a change of heart, Christian conduct, and Scriptural faith.

Sec. 5. Excluded members may be restored to membership upon confessing their errors and giving evidence of repentance.

Sec. 6. No person shall be received as a member of this church if five members object to his or her admission.

ART. II. General Duties of Members

Sec. 1. The duties of members to *themselves* are: the acquisition of Scriptural knowledge; constant progress in spirituality; consistency of external conduct; and the control and eradication of every unholy temper.

Sec. 2. It is the duty of members to honor, esteem, and love their *pastor*; to pray for their pastor fervently and daily; to submit to the Scriptural exercise of pastoral authority; to attend constantly upon the pastor's ministrations; to manifest a tender regard for the pastor's reputation; and to contribute toward the pastor's support in proportion to their ability.

Sec. 3. It is the duty of each member to cultivate and cherish Christian love for all other members of the church and to show this love by using all proper measures to promote their spiritual benefit and prosperity.

Sec. 4. Toward those who are not connected with the church, it is the duty of members to be exact in fulfilling obligations and performing promises; and as opportunity and ability may enable, to commend the gospel of Christ unto them.

Sec. 5. It is the duty of all members removing from the vicinity of the church, to take letters of dismission to other churches of the same denomination; but should this not be practicable, to furnish their names and places of residence within three months after leaving the church.

ART. III. Officers of the Church

Sec. 1. As often as it may be deemed necessary, by the death or removal of a previous pastor, the church shall, without unnecessary delay, invite to its pastorship some minister of good report, provided at least three-fourths of the members present and voting at any meeting, of which two weeks public notice shall have been given, consent to the invitation.

It shall be the duty of the pastor to preach statedly at the church; to administer the ordinances of the gospel; to act as moderator, when present, in meetings for the transaction of business; and to perform the various other duties incumbent on the office.

Sec. 2. The church shall elect deacons by a majority of at least three-fourths of its members present at any regular or duly notified meeting, as often as it may be rendered necessary.

It shall be the duty of the deacons to seek out any members of the church who need financial assistance and to use the alms of the church for their relief; to visit the sick; to prepare and distribute the elements of the Lord's Supper; to take a general supervision of the temporal interests of the church; and to cooperate with and assist the pastor in the performance of his or her duties.

The ordination of deacons shall be preceded by one year's trial. They shall continue in office as long as satisfaction shall be given.

Sec. 3. Seven trustees, a treasurer, a clerk, and a sexton, shall on the _____ in January of every year, be elected by ballot by a majority of votes. In case of any omission to hold the election as above, the election shall be held at the next regular meeting for business. In case of the death, resignation, or removal of any of those officers, an election shall be held to fill the vacancy at the first regular meeting following the former meeting at which such vacancy was announced.

Sec. 4. It shall be the duty of the treasurer to receive all moneys and pay all orders drawn on him or her by order of the church.

The treasurer shall keep a true and fair book of accounts, and annually at the said meeting for business in January, shall lay before the church a statement of the moneys so received and paid, which a committee appointed by the church shall examine with the necessary vouchers.

Sec 5. The clerk shall keep a fair record of the proceedings of the church in their meetings for business; sign all orders on the treasury passed by the church; take charge of all the records; and keep a register of all the members of this church.

ART. IV. Meetings of the Church

Sec. 1. The regular meetings for business shall be held

_____.

Sec. 2. Special meetings may be called by the pastor; or in the pastor's absence, the clerk shall call such a meeting on a written request signed by no fewer than seven members; and the notice shall be publicly given from the pulpit on the Lord's Day preceding.

Sec. 3. Nine members shall constitute a quorum for the transaction of business.

Sec. 4. The church shall regularly meet every Lord's Day, for the public worship of Almighty God.

Sec. 5. The ordinance of the Lord's Supper shall be observed by the church upon _____.

Sec. 6. Once each week, at least, it shall be the duty of the members to meet for prayer.

ART. V. Manner of Conducting Business

Sec. 1. The pastor of the church (or in the pastor's absence, any member whom the church may appoint) shall act as moderator in all meetings for the transaction of business.

Sec. 2. It shall be the duty of the moderator to keep order and to state and explain propositions.

Sec. 3. The moderator shall cause every meeting to be opened and closed by prayer.

Sec. 4. The moderator shall call for the business of the church in the following order:

1. Read the minutes of the previous meeting.

2. Hear the experience of candidates for membership.

3. Receive letters of dismission from sister churches.

4. Grant letters of dismission to those requesting them.

5. Hear reports of committees and other unfinished business.

6. Hear new business.

Sec. 5. The moderator shall suffer no second motion to be entertained until the one under consideration has been disposed of, except motions to amend, postpone, adjourn, or put the main question.

Sec. 6. The moderator shall call to order any member who, while speaking, introduces any subject foreign to the one under discussion.

Sec. 7. The moderator shall call to order any member who uses discourteous language or whose remarks are adapted to injure the reputation or feelings of any other member.

Sec. 8. The moderator may speak upon any subject under discussion by inviting another member to preside in his or her place.

Sec. 9. Every member who wishes to speak shall rise and respectfully address the moderator.

Sec. 10. Every proposition presented for the action of the church must be introduced by the motion of one member—in writing, if requested—and seconded by another.

Sec. 11. No member shall speak more than twice upon the same subject without the expressed consent of the church.

Sec. 12. Upon any point of order a member may appeal from the moderator to the church, whose decision shall be final.

Sec. 13. All questions shall be decided by the vote of a majority, except the cases mentioned in other sections of these rules.

ART. VI. *Mode of Proceeding Against a Disorderly Member*

Sec. 1. When offense is given to one member of the church by the language or conduct of another, if the offense relates only to that one person and is known to none other, the offended shall, without consulting or informing any person, seek opportunity to converse privately with the offender with an honest view to reconcile the difficulty if possible. If satisfaction be given, the offended shall complain of the offender to none.

Sec. 2. If satisfaction is not given, it shall be the duty of the offended to select one or two, or at most three others, choosing such as he or she may deem best adapted to effect a reconciliation, with whom the offended shall again privately converse with the offending person; if satisfaction be given, no further complaint should be made.

Sec. 3. If these efforts fail to secure a reconciliation, it shall be the duty of the offended to lay the matter before the church for further action.

Sec. 4. If any member of the church shall be publicly guilty of any crime or gross impropriety, it shall be the duty of the member knowing the transgression to see or write to the offender and inform him or her of the intention to lay the matter before the church so that the offender may appear in his or her own defense.

Sec. 5. When common rumor charges a crime or gross impropriety against a member, it shall be the duty of any member hearing that rumor to visit or write to the accused and inform him or her of the reports. If the member has reason to believe that the rumor is true, it is his or her duty to take the most judicious steps to ascertain its correctness and lay the charge and its evidence before the church.

Sec. 6. When peculiar circumstances render it impracticable to visit or write to a member who is known or currently reported to have been guilty of crime or gross impropriety, it shall be the duty of the member knowing or hearing of such conduct to take the most judicious measures to ascertain the truth and lay the matter before the church.

Sec. 7. If a member, having erred, shall voluntarily confess it to the church and manifest repentance, no further proceedings, except in cases of public scandal, shall be entertained against him or her.

Sec. 8. If a charge be preferred against an absent member, he or she shall, if practicable, be cited to appear at the next meeting of the church; and no absent member shall be censured or excluded at the same meeting during which a charge is preferred against him or her.

Sec. 9. Every member against whom a charge of misconduct is preferred shall have the privilege of speaking in his or her own defense.

Sect. 10. Written testimony of any individual who is not a member of the church may be admitted in cases of discipline, but no oral testimony shall be admitted unless the individual testifying is connected with some church of the same faith and order.

Sec. 11. If a member fails to give satisfaction to the church in relation to charges preferred against him or her, or perversely refuses to appear before the church when cited, that member shall be excluded.

ART. VII. Convening a Council

In cases of difficulty, for the decision of which the church desires the advice and wisdom of disinterested parties, letters may be sent to the neighboring churches, requesting them to appoint delegates to meet a delegation from the church on a specified day; to which council, when organized, the case shall be referred, and their advice shall be laid before the church for further action.

ART. VIII. Representation in Association

Once in each year delegates shall be appointed to represent the church in the Association; whose duty it shall be to furnish to the Association a statement of the condition of the church, including its changes; to represent faithfully the desires of the church; and to cooperate with the messengers of other churches in advancing the kingdom of Christ.

ART. IX. *Licensing and Ordaining*

Sec. 1. Any member who, in the judgment of the church, gives evidence by piety, zeal, and "aptness to teach" of being called by God to the work of the ministry, after having preached in the hearing of the church, may be licensed to preach the gospel of Jesus Christ, provided three-fourths of the members present at any regular meeting shall agree thereto.
Sec. 2. If the church unanimously decides that one of its licensed preachers possesses the Scriptural qualifications for full ordination, it shall call a council of ministers and members to examine the qualification of the candidate, to which council the propriety of ordaining shall be wholly referred.

ART. X. *Benevolent Action*

The church holds it to be its imperative duty to assist in making known the gospel throughout the world, and will maintain some system by which all the leading objects of Christian benevolence may receive their share of support, and all the members contribute, as the Lord prospers them.
All collections granted to churches, societies, or individu-

als, shall be counted by the deacons before paying over the same; and the amount so collected shall be reported at the next church meeting.

Forms of Church Letters

I. Letter of Dismission

Philadelphia, _____, 19__

To the _____ Baptist Church in _____:

This certifies that ___ ___ is a member in good standing of the First Baptist Church, and in compliance with ____ own request, is affectionately recommended and dismissed to your fellowship.

If notified within six months, of ___ union with you, we shall consider ___ as dismissed from us; otherwise this letter shall be null and void.

In behalf of the church,

_____ _____, Clerk

II. Letter of Notification

To the First Baptist Church, Philadelphia:

This certifies that ____ ___, recommended and dismissed by you by a letter dated ____, was on ____ received as a member of the _____ Baptist Church in _____.

Attest: _____ _____, Clerk

III. Letter of Occasional Communion

_____ _____, 19__

This may certify that the bearer, ____ ___, is a member of

the _____ Baptist Church, in good and regular standing, and as such is affectionately commended to the sympathy, watchcare, and communion of any sister church where Providence may lead _____.

This letter continues valid only one year.

_____ _____, Pastor

IV. A License to Preach

This may certify that the bearer, _____ _____, is a member without reproach of the _____ Baptist Church in _____, and has the full and cordial approbation of the Church, by a vote passed _____, to exercise the bearer's gifts in preaching the gospel of Christ.

Attest: _____ _____, Pastor

_____ _____, Clerk

V. Letter of Dismission to Form a New Church

The _____ Baptist Church, during a regular church meeting on _____, 19__, received a request from the following brothers and sisters (the names are listed here), all of whom are now in regular standing with us, to be dismissed from us for the purpose of uniting in the formation of a new church at _____. It was voted that we cordially grant them letters of dismission for that purpose, and when they are regularly constituted as a church, we shall cease to regard them as under our watchcare.

_____ _____, Clerk

Life Income Agreements

(Formerly Annuities)

You may choose to support any denominational mission or ministry by funding a life income agreement through the appropriate denominational agency. This type of "deferred gift" is available only upon your death or your beneficiary's death. Included are annuities, pooled income funds, and charitable remainder trusts. Some forms of planned gifts may actually increase the value of your assets through improved earnings and possible tax deductions. Contact the appropriate agency in your denomination for complete information.

Wills

A carefully thought-out and well-planned will is a final statement of one's life work. After providing for family and loved ones, many Christians use their wills to express gratitude for a lifetime of blessings. Gifts through your will can be stated as a certain amount, a percentage of your assets, or the naming of a specific property. A will is a legal document; it should be drafted by an attorney based on your instructions. If you are considering a bequest, be sure to get the exact name of the church, region, seminary, national mission board, or denominational organization you wish to benefit. Many denominations have a particular agency that you can contact for information and assistance.